Canterbury
Tale by Tale
by Julian Ng

A Pictorial Sojourn Into Canterbury's Rich History and Heritage

graph by Dr Brenden Tempest-Mogg

Acknowledgements

This book is a labour of love which began out of need. There seemed to be a dearth of simple quick and handy reference guides to Canterbury. Hence, I wrote this book so that anyone can use it, be they tourists, students, or residents wanting to impress with their local knowledge.

This book would not have been possible were it not for the many scholars and Canterbury enthusiasts before me. Research took the form of books and websites, and the ever helpful advice of Yvonne Leach, Blue Badge Guide extraodinaire.

Thanks go to my family and friends also, who have unconditionally put up with my inhospitable working hours and mood swings, and Dr Brenden Tempest-Mogg of Warnborough College for some jaw-droppingly fantastic photographs.

This book is part of the 'I Love Canterbury' Project. For more information, visit **www.ilovecanterbury.co.uk**

References (with thanks)

Bax, S. "Canterbury Buildings"
http://tinyurl.com/6e3xue9

British History Online
http://british-history.ac.uk

The Canterbury Trust
http://www.canterburytrust.co.uk

Collinson, P. "The Canterbury Tour"
http://tinyurl.com/6kro5py

Kent Resources
http://kentresources.co.uk

Machado, T. "Historic Canterbury"
http://www.machadoink.com

Sullivan, M.A.
http://tinyurl.com/6a5cm6f

Visit Canterbury
http://www.canterbury.co.uk

© 2011 Julian Ng. First edition. Published by Warnborough Publishing.
ISBN Number: 978-0-9568667-1-4

**WARNBOROUGH
PUBLISHING**

Table of Contents

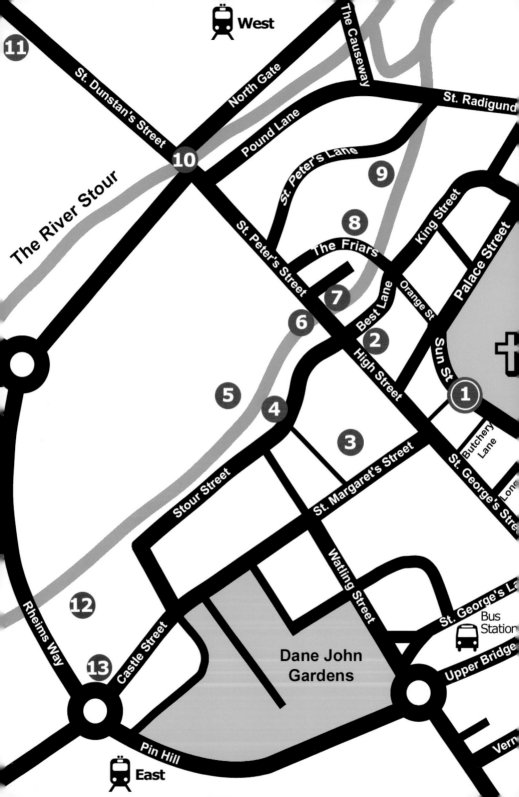

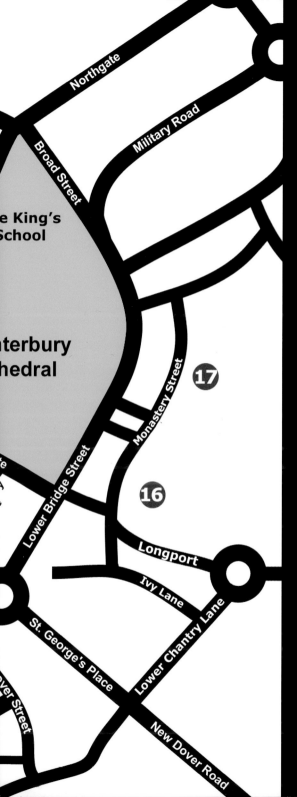

MAP OF CANTERBURY

1. Buttermarket, Tourist Information Centre
2. Beaney Institute and Royal Museum
3. The Canterbury Tales
4. Museum of Canterbury
5. Franciscan Friary
6. Eastbridge Hospital
7. The Old Weavers' House, River Tours
8. The Marlowe Theatre
9. Dominican Friary
10. Westgate Tower
11. St Dunstan's Church
12. St Mildred's Church
13. Canterbury Castle
14. St Thomas Church
15. St George's Clock Tower
16. St Augustine's Abbey
17. Canterbury Christchurch University

Foreword

Julian Ng has produced a superb pocket guidebook, which combines photographs and maps of today's Canterbury with fascinating facts and insights into this beautiful city's past.

Whether on a first visit to Britain's premiere cathedral city, or enjoying a one of many happy returns here, this guide provides a quick snapshot of Canterbury and all that it offers.

No other city in Britain combines so many fascinating features from such a long passage of history, all within a few minutes' walk – and walking is an attractive option, whether you are following in the footsteps of centuries of pilgrims as you explore the Cathedral and its cloisters, tracing the banks of the Stour or admiring the Dane John park.

This book provides you with a huge wealth of ideas of what to see and do and points of interest at every turn.

Julian Brazier, T.D., M.P.
Canterbury

How to Use this Book

Treat this book like a quick walking tour through the history of the city, stopping at the most popular sites. Start at the Tourist Information Centre at the Butter Market, and then work your way through the rest of the book. A timeline shows you the major events in the history of Canterbury. At the end of the book are listings and contact details of the featured attractions and sights.

I hope this book will help you find your way around my beloved city, and that you will grow to love it as much as I do. If you already know Canterbury, use this book as refresher to rediscover all that you love about her.

Canterbury at a Glance

Canterbury is located in the County of Kent (affectionately known as the Garden of England), 62.8 miles southeast of London.

Getting Around: Canterbury is served by two railway stations (Canterbury East and Canterbury West). The high-speed train from Canterbury West gets passengers into London St Pancras in 56 minutes. Tourists can get to Europe on the Eurostar trains from Ashford or Ebbsfleet, via Canterbury West. Canterbury is well-connected by road to London (the M2 and M20 connect to the M25 motorway) and the coastal towns of Dover, Folkestone (A2), Ramsgate and Margate (A28) provide access to and from the continent via ferries.

Eating: Canterbury is a foodie's haven, with everything from fast-food chains to organic vegetarian restaurants. Surrounding farmland means fresh food. Eateries, takeaways and restaurants can be found within and without the city walls.

Education: Canterbury boasts of four universities, elite primary and secondary schools, and a host of other educational institutions.

Famous Residents: Many famous people have originated and/or lived in Canterbury including Ian Fleming, Orlando Bloom, Freddie Laker, Mary Tourtel, Mary Quant, Joseph Conrad, and Somerset Maugham.

History and Timeline

Canterbury – a seat of power, fought over by kings and queens through the centuries. It is not very big, not particularly industrious. However, the stories it tells have filled bookshelves the world over. Here is a snippet of Canterbury's history over the last 2000 years.

Time	Event
Pre 1AD	Belgic tribe known as the Cantiaci settle here.
43	Romans capture and rename the town to 'Durovernum Cantiacorum' (Cantiaci stronghold by the alder grove).
280	Romans build a massive wall around the city. Over the centuries, there would eventually be seven city gates.
410	Romans leave Britain. Anglo Saxons and Danes take over the settlement, renaming it 'Cantwaraburh' (Stronghold of Kent).
597	Augustine is sent by Pope Gregory I to convert England to Christianity. King Æthelbert of Canterbury gives him land to build an abbey and a cathedral. Canterbury becomes the Episcopal see for Kent and Augustine, its first Archbishop.
672	Canterbury is a bustling centre of trade with its own mint. The see of Canterbury is given authority over the entire English Church.
851	Constant Danish raids kill many.
978	Archbishop Dunstan rebuilds and renames St Augustine's Abbey.
1011	The Cathedral is razed and Archbishop Alphege killed by Danes when he refuses to allow a ransom to be paid for his freedom. Thorkell the Tall who led the Danes is so incensed by his fellowmen's cruelty, he defects to the English.
1066	William I, the Norman, invades and takes over Canterbury. It would be the last time that Britain was conquered by a foreign power. A wooden motte and bailey castle is erected (it is later rebuilt in stone).
1072	Canterbury is designated as the supreme archdiocese in England.
1077	The first Norman Archbishop, Lanfranc rebuilds and dedicates the Cathedral.
1162	Thomas Becket becomes Archbishop of Canterbury.
1170	Becket is murdered by 4 knights. Canterbury becomes a centre of pilgrimage.
1174	Henry II makes a penitential pilgrimage to Canterbury. The Cathedral is consumed by fire again and is rebuilt after 1175.

Time	Event
1348	Canterbury is decimated by the Black Death (plague).
1376	The Black Prince, heir to King Edward III, is buried in the Cathedral.
1380s	Geoffrey Chaucer writes and publishes his famous Canterbury Tales.
1448	Canterbury receives a City Charter and its own Mayor and Sheriff.
1520	The Cathedral's Christ Church Gate is completed.
1539	Canterbury Cathedral surrenders after King Henry VIII breaks from Rome to found his own church and disbands all existing monasteries. Becket's shrine is ordered to be destroyed, and all the riches sequestered to the Tower of London. Its abbey is turned into the Kings School.
1558	The last Catholic Archbishop of Canterbury, Cardinal Pole, dies.
1564	Christopher Marlowe is baptised in St George's Church.
1567	The first Huguenot weavers fleeing Belgium arrive in Canterbury.
1573	Queen Elizabeth I visits Canterbury and entertains the Duke of Alençon.
1620	Robert Cushman negotiates the lease for the Mayflower to transport the Pilgrims to America.
1642	The English Civil War breaks out. The Cathedral is sacked by the Puritans.
1717	The Kentish Post becomes Canterbury's first newspaper.
1770	All the city gates except for Westgate are demolished for impeding coach travel.
1830	The Canterbury and Whitstable Railway, the world's first passenger railway opens. Known affectionately as the Crab and Winkle line due to Whitstable's fame for its seafood, it was the first in the world to offer season tickets.
1942	Canterbury comes under attack from German bombers during the Baedecker Blitz. Much of the city is devastated, including parts of the Cathedral.
1962	The University of Kent is established.
1982	Pope John Paul II visits Canterbury.
1997	Canterbury receives its own radio station.
2003	The present Archbishop of Canterbury, Rowan Williams, is appointed.
2004	The Canterbury Archaeological Trust goes on the 'Big Dig' after which the Whitefriars shopping complex is developed.
2011	The new Marlowe Theatre opens.

The Buttermarket

We begin here, at the **Buttermarket** – an 800-year old square that once housed a covered market. In the square stands a **Memorial** dedicated in 1921 to soldiers who fell in World War I.

Two centuries ago, the square was known as '*Bullstake*'. Bull-baiting was a gambling sport where bulls would be tied to a big iron stake, with bulldogs (what else?) set upon them to try and bite their snouts. Locals would watch and bet on this grisly entertainment (well, there was no TV or Internet then). Also, they beat the bulls in the belief that this tenderised the steak.

Here too is the majestic **Christ Church Gate**, the main entrance into the Canterbury Cathedral precinct. Completed sometime between 1502 and 1520, it was probably a tribute to King Henry VIII's brother, Arthur (who was supposed to be King), and his wife, Katherine of Aragon (Henry married her after Arthur's death). Carved on the gate are little heads of Arthur

Photograph of The Buttermarket by Dr Brenden Tempest-Mogg

and Katherine, plus the royal arms of the nobility present at the wedding. During the Civil War in the 1600s, Oliver Cromwell's Parliamentarians damaged much of the Gate, using the central statue of Christ as target practice. Eventually, the statue was pulled down and smashed. A modern bronze figure of a welcoming Christ was erected in its place in 1991.

The **Cathedral Gate Hotel** beside is actually older than the gate. Built in 1438, it was called the 'Sonne Hospice' – this name later moved to a different inn on Sun Street (where Charles Dickens once stayed).

The **Canterbury Tourist Information Centre** is located opposite. Get information on (and book) tours and accommodation here.

Canterbury Cathedral

Pope Gregory I sent Augustine in 597 AD to convert the Anglo Saxons to Christianity. He landed at Ebbsfleet before making his way to Canterbury.

King Æthelbert, the king of Kent, was a pagan. His wife Bertha, a Christian Frankish princess, worshipped at St Martin's Church. At her behest, he received Augustine and his monks, and gave them land on which to build an abbey and a cathedral.

Augustine built his Anglo-Saxon style cathedral using reused Roman bricks and mortared stone. It was completed in 602 AD. Archbishop Dunstan had the cathedral rebuilt as a much larger structure In the 10th century.

Danish raiders led by Thorkell the Tall plundered and burnt the city in 1011. The Cathedral was badly damaged, and it did not survive a fire in 1067.

After the Norman conquest in 1066, Lanfranc became the first Norman archbishop. He rebuilt the Cathedral in the style of St Etienne Abbey in Caen. It was dedicated in 1077.

The Cathedral entered history books permanently in 1170 with the murder of *Thomas á Becket*, the 40th Archbishop of Canterbury. King Henry II had installed his best friend, Becket, in the primacy in the hope that he would lessen the influence and independence of the Church. However, Becket became an ascetic and directly contradicted Henry. In exasperation,

Henry was rumoured to have exclaimed "Will no one rid me of this troublesome priest?"

Four of his knights took it to mean that he wanted Becket dead. They journeyed from France and asked for an audience with Becket. When Becket refused their demands, they returned and cut him down with swords.

Becket was made a saint in 1173. His shrine at the Cathedral became an important medieval site of pilgrimage. Henry II, who was widely blamed for Becket's murder, did a public penance at the shrine in 1174. The pilgrims came for several hundred years until 1538 when King Henry VIII ordered the shrine and Becket's bones to be destroyed. All the gold was removed to the Tower of London. Under Catholic law, Henry VIII was not allowed to divorce, so he created his own church, dissolved the existing Catholic monasteries, and claimed their riches for his own.

In the 1640s, the Civil War broke out and the Cathedral suffered much damage. When it ended, the Cathedral underwent major repairwork. The ruined Northwest Tower was deemed dangerous, and demolished in the 1830s. It was replaced by a copy of the Southwest Tower.

More recently, during World War II, the Cathedral's library was destroyed and the Precincts were heavily damaged. Painstaking ongoing repair work greets visitors today.

Next to it, you will see the flint **St Alphege Church** (now the Canterbury Environment Centre). The Rectory House used to stand behind the wall, but it was demolished in 1876. The little doorway in the wall used to lead directly to the Rectory, and dates back to the 13th century. **3**

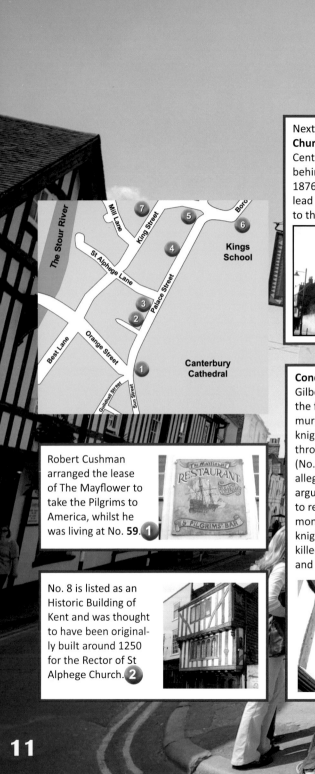

Robert Cushman arranged the lease of The Mayflower to take the Pilgrims to America, whilst he was living at No. **59**. **1**

No. 8 is listed as an Historic Building of Kent and was thought to have been originally built around 1250 for the Rector of St Alphege Church. **2**

Conquest House (No. 17) was owned by Gilbert the Citizen in 1170. It is said that the four knights rested here before they murdered Thomas Becket. Two of the knights entered the Cathedral Precincts through the Archbishop's Palace entrance (No. 41). Becket would not renounce his allegiance to a supreme God. After a heated argument, they returned to Conquest House to retrieve their weapons. Although the monks tried to persuade Becket to hide, the knights stormed into the Cathedral. They killed Becket by cutting off part of his head and spilling some of his brains on the floor.

4

Palace Street

Re-developed into a pedestrianised shopping area known as the King's Mile, Palace Street harbours quite a few historical gems among its restaurants and shops.

The Old King's School Shop, lovingly known as the '**Crooked House**'. The 17th century building started leaning after a doorway was put into the central chimney stack, which weakened it. **5**

Palace Street curves into the Borough. Here is the entrance to the **King's School**. Originally an abbey with formal teaching, the School is claimed to have been founded by St Augustine in 597 AD (making it the world's oldest school). It was renamed and re-purposed after Henry VIII annexed all the church buildings and removed the monks. **6**

Veer back left onto King Street, and you will see the site of the chantry where the Black Prince housed monks. Beside it is the very first synagogue in Canterbury (circa 12th century). It is now the *King's School Music Conservatory*. **7**

A River Runs Through It

The beautiful river Stour runs through and around Canterbury, creating a little island in the middle of the city. Many noteworthy sites dot the river.

1 Dominican Priory. Founded in 1237 by 13 Dominican monks, it was surrendered to the Bishop of Dover in 1538 on Henry VIII's orders before being let, then sold off, to various tenants. Most of the Priory was demolished by the 1800s.

2 The Marlowe Theatre. Began life in the 1920s as a cinema and a repertory theatre. It was refurbished in 1984 only for the use of theatre productions and closed in 2009. It was demolished and a new modern theatre opens in summer 2011.

3 The Westgate Tower. Originally part of the City Walls and the main entrance into Canterbury, it was built by Archbishop Sudbury in 1380. It is the largest surviving city gate in England and has been used as a prison, and is now a museum.

4 The Westgate Gardens. Picturesquely charming with punting on the Stour, a 200 year old oriental plane tree, and a Norman archway. Relax with swans, ducks and moor-hens in perfectly manicured gardens.

5 **Eastbridge Hospital**. 'Hospitality' derives from the name - it was founded in 1190 to provide accommodation for weary pilgrims. It was a boys' school for over 300 years.

6 **The Weavers**. Built to house Huguenot weavers who fled religious persecution in France or Flanders in the late 1500s. Their looms boomed Canterbury's economy until the 1800s when cheaper Indian silk and the northern factories killed the industry.

7 **Museum of Canterbury**. Housed in the medieval Poor Priests' Hospital, it showcases exhibits from pre-Roman times until the present. The Rupert Bear Museum is here.

8 **The Greyfriars Monastery and Gardens**. The oldest Franciscan monastery in England was built in 1267. Greyfriars Chapel is the only remaining structure and its gardens are still maintained by Franciscan monks staying at Eastbridge Hospital. Mass is still said here.

9 **Watling Street**. The original 'highway' from Canterbury to St Albans, paved by the Romans. Geoffrey Chaucer mentions Watling Street in his famous Tales, describing the pilgrims' journey from Southwark to Canterbury.

Canterbury Castle, Dane Joh

A wooden motte and bailey castle was erected at Dane John soon after the Battle of Hastings in 1066 - probably to guard William of Normandy's route from Dover to London. A later build of the Castle was one of the three original Royal castles of Kent during the reign of Henry I (1100 to 1135).

Under Henry I, a great stone keep (the fifth largest in England) was built. It became the county gaol in the 1200s and was surrendered to the French in the First Barons' War. Part of the castle was demolished in the 1700s to allow access to Castle Street. In 1825, a gas company bought it and demolished more internal walls in order to store coal and coke. The city bought back the castle in 1928 to preserve it.

Gardens and the City Wall

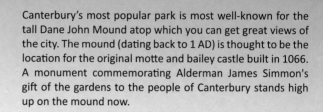

Canterbury's most popular park is most well-known for the tall Dane John Mound atop which you can get great views of the city. The mound (dating back to 1 AD) is thought to be the location for the original motte and bailey castle built in 1066. A monument commemorating Alderman James Simmon's gift of the gardens to the people of Canterbury stands high up on the mound now.

The park dates back to the 1550s, and was fully renovated by the City Council in 1999. With a pavilion and a maze, it is a great place to just relax and have fun. It often plays host to food fairs and music festivals.

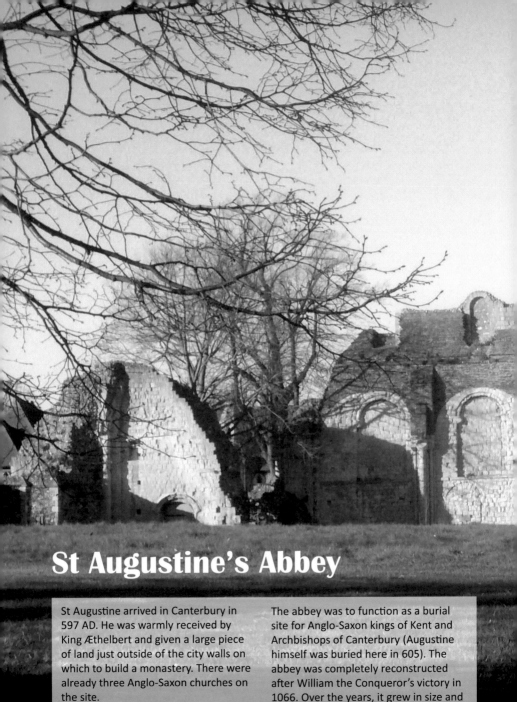

St Augustine's Abbey

St Augustine arrived in Canterbury in 597 AD. He was warmly received by King Æthelbert and given a large piece of land just outside of the city walls on which to build a monastery. There were already three Anglo-Saxon churches on the site.

The abbey was to function as a burial site for Anglo-Saxon kings of Kent and Archbishops of Canterbury (Augustine himself was buried here in 605). The abbey was completely reconstructed after William the Conqueror's victory in 1066. Over the years, it grew in size and

Canterbury Christchurch University

Built on the surrounding land next to St Augustine's Abbey, the university was originally founded as a teacher training college in 1962 by the Church of England to meet the acute shortage of teachers in church schools. It became an official 'university' in 2005, and Dr Rowan Williams, the Archbishop of Canterbury, was inaugurated as its very first Chancellor.

buildings until King Henry VIII decided to split from the Roman Catholic Church in order to marry Anne Boleyn. He ordered all the monasteries to be dissolved and all the monks evicted. The treasures he appropriated for himself. The Abbey was not spared.

Some parts of the abbey were demolished and some parts were converted into a palace for Henry's fourth wife, Anne of Cleves. The palace is thought to have survived until 1703 when a great storm wrought terrible damage.

Burgate

This street is named after the one of the main Roman gates in the walls of Canterbury. The original gate is estimated to have been constructed circa 270 AD. The street was first documented in 1002 AD as 'Burhstraet'. The gate was rebuilt in the 1500s, but was eventually demolished in its entirety by 1822 in order to widen the street.

St Thomas' Church

A relatively modern church (1875) built of ragstone and bathstone on the site of the medieval chapel dedicated to St Mary Magdalen. The tower of the chapel still stands in front of the church. On the right wall of the church is a large stone relief commemorating when Pope Gregory I met with a blond Anglian slave boy - it was this meeting which led Pope Gregory to send St Augustine to convert pagan England. In the frontal buttress of the church is a seven-foot stone statue of St Thomas Becket, flanked by two angels.

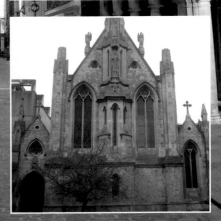

Butchery Lane

It has been documented that there was a Shambles (old English for meat or fish market) off Burgate Street. This is why the site of many a butcher's stall is now called Butchery Lane.

The Roman Museum

This unique underground museum is built around the excavated remains of an original Roman townhouse with mosaic floors. Everyday Roman life is painstakingly recreated, including a scene from a Roman market, and a sword burial.

Full Circle

Continuing down Burgate Street will lead you back to the Buttermarket and the Canterbury Tourist Information Centre. This completes your walking tour of Canterbury. Hopefully, history came alive for you as it does for hundreds of people in Canterbury each day.

Other Places of Interest

There are other places of interest in Canterbury, some just a little further from the city centre.

Beaney Institute & Royal Museum

Opened in 1899, it was built on funds bequeathed by Dr JG Beaney of Melbourne. It incorporates the city's library, an art gallery, natural history displays, and the Buffs Regimental Museum (*main picture*).

St George's Clock Tower

The only remains of an 11th century church dedicated to St George the Martyr, it was bombed in 1942 during the infamous Baedecker Raids. The well-known dramatist, Christopher Marlowe, was baptised here.

St Mildred's Church

This is the only surviving pre-Norman church inside the city walls and has been in continuous use since Saxon times. It features a beamed roof dating back to the 1300s, and medieval woodcarvings.

Photograph of The Beaney Institute & Royal Museum by Dr Brenden Tempest-Mogg

Marlowe Statue
Born in Canterbury in 1564, Christopher Marlowe was a shoemaker's son. He studied at the Kings School before going on to Cambridge. He is considered one of the most important English dramatists before Shakespeare. He was murdered in Deptford in 1593.

St Martin's Church
This is the oldest church in continuous use in the English-speaking world. It was the private chapel of Queen Bertha of Kent in the 6th century, and Augustine set up his mission here. It is claimed that some parts date back to the late Roman period (4th/5th century).

St Dunstan's Church
Dating back to the late 900s, it was rededicated when St Dunstan was canonised in 1003. King Henry II started his penitential pilgrimage to Thomas Becket's shrine here in 1170. Sir Thomas More's decapitated head is in the Roper family vault.

Fordwich (Fordewicum)

A former Roman settlement, it is the smallest town in Britain. In the Middle Ages, it was the main port for Canterbury. The estuary has since silted up and Thanet is no longer an island. The ancient St Mary the Virgin church (now redundant) contains part of a sarcophagus rumoured to have housed Saint Augustine's relics. The smallest town hall in England is in Fordwich.

Whitstable

8km from Canterbury, on the seafront, Whitstable is famous for its oysters. The town pre-dates the Domesday Book. The world's first steam passenger and freight railways service was opened between Whitstable and Canterbury in 1830.

Herne Bay

A small pretty seaside town (with a 2km shingle beach) that rose to prominence in the Victorian era as a health resort, Herne Bay had the UK's second longest pier and the world's first free-standing clock tower. The Herne Bay Festival every August showcases music, art and talent.

Reculver

Situated 3 miles from Herne Bay, Reculver was a strategic location for the Romans, who built a fort there. An Anglo-Saxon palace was rumoured to have replaced the fort. However, what remains are the ruins of a monastery, whose distinctive twin spires (known as the 'Twin Sisters') were used as marine landmarks. The Reculver shoreline was also used to test the Barnes Wallis' 'bouncing bombs' which were subsequently used on Germany in WWII. *See main picture.*

Photograph of the Reculver Twin Sisters by Dr Brenden Tempest-Mogg

Other Activities

Canterbury Walking Tours
Book these tours by official city guides at the Tourist Information Centre.

Canterbury Ghost Tour
Take a scary descent into history with Canterbury's own Ghost Hunter.

The Canterbury Tales
A reconstruction of Chaucer's medieval England, located in the historic (former) St Margaret's Church.

Historic River Tours
Learn about Canterbury's history from a completely different perspective. Drift gently under centuries-old buildings on a river that has seen it all.

Canterbury Punting Company
Relax on a traditional hand-built flat boat while expert tour guides push gently along with wooden poles telling you Canterbury tales.

Shopping, Galleries, Antique Shops
Canterbury rivals most cities in terms of the selection of shops, from small family crafts to big retail names. Scour the nooks and crannies of Canterbury's ancient streets to find bargains, antiques and fine art.

Useful Listings

While all effort has been made to ensure that the details below are accurate, please check the respective websites for up-to-date information, opening times, and prices.*

Canterbury Audio Tour (Kent Tours Ltd)
19 Burgate, Canterbury, CT1 2HG
Tel: 01227 767 543
www.tourist-tracks.com/tours/
canterbury.html

Canterbury Cathedral
The Precincts, Canterbury, CT1 2EH
Tel: 01227 762 862
www.canterbury-cathedral.org
Times: Mon – Sat, 09:00 - 17:00
        Sun, 12:30 - 14:30

Canterbury Ghost Tour
38 St Margaret's Street, Outside
Alberry's, Canterbury, CT1 2TY
Tel: 0845 519 0267
www.canterburyghosttour.com
Times: Fri and Sat, 20:00

Canterbury Historic River Tours
Kings Bridge, St Peter's Street,
Canterbury, CT1 2AT
www.canterburyrivertours.co.uk
Times: Daily, 10:00 – 17:00

Canterbury Norman Castle
Castle Street, Canterbury, CT1 2PR
Tel: 01227 378 100
Times: Daily, morning – dusk

Canterbury Punting Company
Water Lane, Canterbury, CT1 2NQ
www.canterburypunting.co.uk
Times: Daily, 10:00 – 17:00

Canterbury Roman Museum
Butchery Lane, Canterbury, CT1 2JR
Tel: 01227 785 575
www.canterbury-museums.co.uk
Times: Mon – Sat, 10:00 – 16:00
        Sun, 11:00 – 15:00

The Canterbury Tales
St Margaret's Street, Canterbury, CT1 2TG
Tel: 01227 479 227
www.canterburytales.org.uk
Times: Daily, 10:00 – 17:00

Canterbury Tourist Guides
Tel: 01227 459 779
www.canterbury-walks.co.uk
Times: Daily, from 11:00

Canterbury Visitor Centre
12-13 Sun Street, Canterbury, CT1 2HX
Tel: 01227 378 100
Fax: 01227 378 101
www.canterbury.co.uk
Times: Mon – Sat, 09:30 - 17:00
        Sun, 09:30 - 16:30

Dane John Gardens
Watling Street, Canterbury, CT1 2RN
Tel: 01227 378 100

Dominican Priory
off St Peter's Street, Canterbury, CT1 2BG

Eastbridge Hospital
25 High Street, Canterbury, CT1 2BD
Tel: 01227 471 688
www.eastbridgehospital.org.uk
Times: Mon – Sat, 10:00 – 17:00

Fordwich Town Hall
King Street, Fordwich, CT2 0DA
Tel: 01227 710 326
www.fordwich.net
Times: Check website as dates change.

Greyfriars Chapel
Next to 6 Stour Street, Canterbury, CT1 2NR
Tel: 01227 471 688
www.eastbridgehospital.org.uk
Times: Daily

The Marlowe Theatre
12 – 13 Sun Street, Canterbury, CT1 2HX
Tel: 01227 787 787
www.marlowetheatre.com
Times: Check website for details

**Museum of Canterbury
(including Rupert Bear Museum)**
Stour Street, Canterbury, CT1 2NR
Tel: 01227 475 202
www.canterbury-museums.co.uk
Times: Mon – Sat, 10:00 – 16:00
        Sun, 11:00 – 15:00

Old Weavers' House (now a restaurant)
1-3 St. Peters Street
Canterbury CT1 2AT
Tel: 01227 464 660
weaversrestaurant.co.uk

Reculver Country Park & Reculver Towers
Reculver, Herne Bay, CT6 6SS
Tel: 01227 740 676
alturl.com/gep82
Times: Check website, from 11:00

St Augustine's Abbey
Longport, Canterbury, CT1 1PF
Tel: 01227 767 345
www.english-heritage.org.uk/
staugustinesabbey
Times: Check website for details

St Dunstan's Church
80 London Road, Canterbury, CT2 8LS
Tel: 01227 472 557
www.canterburystdunstan.org.uk
Times: Mon – Sat, 10:00 – 16:00
        Sun, 08:00 – 18:00

St Martin's Church
North Holmes Road, Canterbury, CT1 1QJ
Tel: 01227 453 469
www.martinpaul.org
Times: Tue, Thu, Sat, 11:00 – 15:00
        Sun, 09:50 – 10:30

St Mildred's Church
Church Lane, Canterbury, CT1 2PP
Tel: 01227 455 994
www.canterburycityparish.org.uk
Times: Sun, 11:00 service

St Thomas Church
59 Burgate, Canterbury, CT1 2HJ
Tel: 01227 462 896
www.rc.net/southwark/canterbury
Times: Check website for details

The Royal Museum and Art Gallery
18 High Street, Canterbury, CT1 2RA
Tel: 01227 452 747
www.canterbury-museums.co.uk
Times: Check website for details

West Gate Towers Museum
Westgate, Canterbury, CT1 2BQ
Tel: 01227 789 576
www.canterbury-museums.co.uk
Times: Check website for details

Westgate Gardens
Westgate Grove, Canterbury, CT1 2BQ
www.canterbury.gov.uk
Times: Closed at dusk

Clockwise from top: The new Marlowe theatre (p 13) ; the Dane John monument (p 16); the top of Canterbury Castle (p 15); the view of the city from St Martin's Church (p 22)

Above: Charles Dickens used the Sun Hotel as the model for Mr Micawber's Little Inn in David Coperfield.
Below: Canterbury High Street as seen from Westgate. Photographs courtesy of Dr Brenden Tempest-Mogg.